Praise for

"Grace to Administrate"

Grace to Administrate is truly a book of prophetic wisdom and insight on the administration of the Gifts of the Spirit. A must-read! It will revolutionize how you lead others into excellence through servanthood.

>Dr. Vera E. Speed
>City Reachers Int'l. Ministries, Founder & President,
>Ennis, TX

Apostle Dr. Cynthia Chess, a very dear friend, offers an entirely new perspective to the gift and role of an Administrator in her new book, *Grace to Administrate*. She brings out the poignant and significant details that are not commonly acknowledged, recognized, or appreciated about this gift. This is the first book I have read that is thoroughly designed to first and foremost identify the significance of the role of an Administrator, and secondly, to thrust the so often "*hidden-in-the-background administrator*" forward. Because it is such a gift which is often ignored, overlooked, or even taken for granted, the person with this gift sometimes finds it difficult to recognize their own authentic identity.

The role of an Administrator as described in this book encapsulates the role of an apostle, pioneer, and trailblazer rolled into one. I love one of the descriptive phrases Apostle Cynthia uses: "to lead, rule, organize, and govern." She has indeed shed much light for so many people who do not acknowledge this gift, or the person(s) carrying the weightiness of this gift, who have not yet stepped into nor embraced, their true calling or governmental assignment on earth. More than thirty years ago, I knew I was an excellent Administrator, both in the church and the marketplace. I knew I was a pioneer and a trailblazer. However, I only knew apostles existed back in the early church, and there was no one around or books to read, to help me identify my true calling—that of an apostle. So, Apostle Cynthia, I applaud your tenacity in bringing this information to the forefront. It will prove to be a very beneficial tool employing another powerful, authoritative, and effective gift in the Body of Christ and beyond. How exciting it is for a person to finally come into the reality of their purpose and destiny and the reason they were released into the earth during this season.

Apostle Gayle Rogers, PhD.
Forever Free, Inc., Apostolic Coaching for Empowerment LLC, Founder & President, Port Saint Lucie, FL

In this hour of mass-produced leadership that is as wide as an ocean but often only inches deep, it is essential to grab hold of biblical perspectives that produce powerful results.

Leaders are chosen by necessity, found in times of crisis, birthed in fire, formed in pressure, and built by wisdom. But the greatest leaders are crafted by the mind of God and the hand of time, with gifts discovered and cultivated strength.

This book by Dr. Chess pulls out of us wrong thinking, pours into us right alignment, and puts us into defined roles of kingdom advancement that lets the Body take territory, without taking casualties along the way.

Grace to Administrate is a must-read for every leader. Whether in church, business, government, education, or media, take the time to sharpen the skill to administrate for God's perspective. Because if the Lord isn't administrating the building of the house, everyone working will soon be frustrated and produce nothing.

    APOSTLE/PROPHET MICHAEL DALTON
    YES Ministries International, Thousand Palms, CA

GRACE TO ADMINISTRATE

"Wisdom to Operate & Govern Effectively in the Body of Christ"

Apostle Dr. Cynthia L. Chess

in conjunction with **KishKnows Publishing Services**

Grace to Administrate - "Wisdom to Operate & Govern Effectively in the Body of Christ" by Apostle Dr. Cynthia L. Chess

Cover design, editing, book layout, and publishing services by KishKnows, Inc., Richton Park, Illinois, 708-252-DOIT

admin@kishknows.com, www.kishknows.com

ISBN 978-0-578-63746-4

LCCN 2020901035

All rights reserved. No part of this book may be reproduced, distributed, or transmitted in any form or by any means, including photocopying, recording, digital scanning, or other electronic or mechanical methods, without the prior written permission of the publisher, except in the case of brief quotations embodied in critical reviews and certain other noncommercial uses permitted by copyright law. For permission requests, please contact Cynthia Chess at admin@clchess.org

Some Scripture references may be paraphrased versions or illustrative references of the author.

Unless otherwise indicated, all Scripture quotations are taken from the **New King James Version®** **(NKJV)**. Copyright © 1982 by Thomas Nelson. Used by permission. All rights reserved.

Copyright © 2019 by Cynthia L. Chess

Printed in the United States of America

Special Recognition and Dedication to…

My Wonderful Family

My husband, Troy, who is my greatest spiritual and emotional supporter.

My son, Joy, and my amazing grandchildren: Kharma and Loyal, for your patience and understanding.

My sister, Tina Williams, for your gracious support and love.

Special Friends

My bishop, spiritual mother, mentor, and dear friend, Dr. Ernestine Cleveland Reems, for the seeds you have sown and the impartation you have made in my life.

My friend and instructor, Dr. Brenda Wright, for the depth of insight and wisdom you have released over me.

My dear friend in the gospel, the late Apostle Alonzo Wade, for his encouragement.

My spiritual daughter, Rachel Coicou, for cheering me on to the finish line.

My fabulous church family, Mountain's Hope Community Worship Center, for allowing me to be your Moses, and for holding up my arms throughout this process.

I sincerely love and appreciate you all!

Preface

As one who has the Gift of Administration, I have chosen to write on the subject *Grace to Administrate* because I have seen and experienced those in the Body of Christ who have abused this gift. Many have not been able to distinguish between *true administration* and a *religious spirit*. I'd like for all to understand what this gift looks like, its purpose, and the necessity of grace. Those who house this gift must appreciate *why* they see what they see, both natural and spiritual, and *what to do* with what they see. In addition, one must determine if their visual perception is from a religious spirit or an administrative advantage. The difference is that administrative advantage brings resolution while a religious spirit brings judgment and condemnation.

The Gift of Administration is the ability to lead, rule, organize, and govern; and in doing so, there is spiritual insight given to understand the "overall picture, program, and process of any given situation." Those who operate with this gift will most certainly "get the job done," however, we must be careful not to do this while losing and wounding precious souls in the process. If one does not operate with grace in this gift, they can become haughty, cynical, judgmental, and critical. If not aware of the grace to administrate, it may even be possible for them to become discouraged to the point of giving up or causing others to give up.

Table of Contents

1. The Gift of Administration 1

   ## Administration and Servanthood

2. Jesus Knew Who He Was 15
3. Jesus Knew Whose He Was 21
4. Jesus Knew His Purpose 29

   ## Administration and the Oil of Anointing

5. Oil for Your Purpose 37
6. Authentic Anointing vs. Counterfeit Anointing 41
7. Owning Your Oil 49
8. Using Your Oil 53

   ## Administration and Character

9. Think It and Do It 61
10. Everyone Matters 65
11. Administrators Never Retreat—We Fight Back! 73

    ## Administration and Grace

12. Graceful Administration 89

References 101
About the Author 102
Contact the Author 104

1

The Gift of Administration

What is the Gift of Administration?

Have you ever attended a wedding, concert, conference, or meeting and thought any of the following to yourself, or perhaps mentioned it to others?

- "Hmm, if only they would have started with…"
- "That song would have been more appropriate at the end of the program rather than the beginning…"
- "When they did it like that, it was out of context with…"
- "They really should have moved that part of the service to…"

Perhaps you have walked into a place of business such as a hospital, grocery store, or fast food restaurant and said, "If the person working over there were doing what this person is doing, then things would have run more smoothly…" or "They need another person to do…" Do you ever wonder why you see the order of things when others don't? Or why you see the whole picture and the flow from beginning to end? Are you the one who can anticipate the hiccups, strategy, and order in a given situation? It may be that you house the "Gift of Administration."

The Governing Gift

The Gift of Administration is the ability to lead, rule, organize, and govern. In doing so, spiritual insight and eyesight are given to understand and assess the "overall state of affairs," be it spiritual or natural. The Gift of Administration is a governing gift. The one entrusted with this gift is someone who rules and oversees, through understanding function and execution.

> *One with administrative giftings instinctively knows order. They understand how things should flow, when something is out of order, and what it will take to bring things back into order.*

People housing this gift will also recognize giftings, talents, and abilities in others. An Administrator not only recognizes the giftings but will know what to do with them as well. They know who will fit best where in order to accomplish a specific job or task and will know how to strategically place people where they belong, helping them to succeed and achieve their potential. Moves made by an Administrator are strategic, similar to those of a chessboard. Individuals, like the pieces on the board, are strategically placed for the win. This gift sees order and knows execution.

> *"And God has appointed these in the church: first Apostles, second Prophets, third Teachers, after that miracles, then*

gifts of healings, helps, administrations, varieties of tongues."
1 Corinthians 12:28 (NKJV)

According to Strong's #2941 Greek definition, administration comes from the Greek word **kybernēsis**, (pronounced koo-ber'-nay-sis); of Latin origin meaning to steer; pilotage, i.e. (figuratively) directorship (in the church): government.

Steering Through Turbulent Waters

Let's take a look at some of the definitions for **kybernesis**. First is the word "steer." To steer is defined as "to guide, control, or maneuver." The one who steers a vehicle, vessel, or aircraft is the one who will guide and control the movement thereof. For example, a helmsman, by turning the wheel or operating the rudder, will guide a ship to its destination. The helmsman knows how to orchestrate the movement of the ship even through adverse weather conditions and turbulent waters. A good helmsman at the control of the wheel at the right time can literally dictate the survival of a ship.

The primary role of the helmsman is to maintain a steady course. Their principal communication is with the officer on the bridge. This communication is of utmost importance to ensure safe navigation and ship handling. The helmsman is vital to a ship's captain—reaching his purposed goal and destination.

According to many online sources, steering a ship effectively requires skills gained through training and experience. An expert helmsman has a keen sense of how a particular ship will respond to the helm or how different sea conditions might impact the steering. In addition, an expert helmsman also knows how to strategically maneuver a ship through varying degrees of water. He or she knows how to ride up and over the waves, take the waves at the proper angle, and change course if necessary.

At the Helm

How do the skills of a helmsman compare with one who has the Gift of Administration? Similar to an experienced helmsman, one with the Gift of Administration possesses the ability to *control, correct,* and *maintain a steady course* in ministry. This person is able to foresee trouble and instances where things may go wrong or off course. It is with great skill and wisdom that the one with an administrative gifting is able to bring correction and cause the ship to return to its course, all because they have been expertly empowered by the Holy Spirit and have remained in direct communication with the Captain, King Jesus!

This person is skilled and knowledgeable in understanding how various aspects of ministry will respond in diverse spiritual conditions by expertly maneuvering and preventing a ministry from substantially falling off course.

Piloting the Ship

Next, let us explore the word "**pilotage**." As with the helmsman, pilots are "those who guide or direct the course of action for others." An airline pilot operates a plane's engines and controls in order to navigate and fly the vessel. Prior to taking flight, the pilot must file a flight plan, a document that indicates a plane's planned route. Some of the primary content of these plans include information on the pilot, type of aircraft, departure and arrival locations, alternate routes or airports in case of emergency, and the number of passengers anticipated. Although the desire is to have a smooth, turbulence-free flight, airline pilots often anticipate turbulence and are trained to handle it in order to minimize its effects. They also anticipate when to change altitude in search of smoother conditions.

There are times when serious conditions dictate a change in the flight plan. This change occurred with Captain Chesley Burnett "Sully" Sullenberger III. In 2009, the plane in which Captain Sullenberger was flying had both engines damaged after striking a flock of Canada geese, causing the plane to lose power.

Captain Sullenberger realized there was no time to turn back or be redirected to the nearest airport, and so he opted to land US Airways Flight #1549 in the nearest safe place—the Hudson River. Although this was a successful alternate plan, no one could have anticipated this type of landing, nor would anything like this have been included on a flight plan. If it had not been for Captain Sullenberger's faith and wisdom, many (if not all) of the 155 passengers on board would have been killed.

Confidence in Chaos

As with Captain Sullenberger, people with the Gift of Administration have "confidence in chaos" and will look for the "out of the box" alternative when needed. Those with the Gift of Administration anticipate when to change course and understand that there are times when they must take an alternate route. This may mean taking a route never before explored or an alternate route that does not reasonably make sense.

Whatever ministry plan one has in place, turbulence and unforeseen circumstances are bound to occur. The most important thing is that the one with the Gift of Administration must maintain composure and a sense of level-headedness in an effort to navigate and maneuver through the most difficult times.

The Director

Next, let us look at "**directorship**," as it relates to the role of a director of theater and the arts. A director is "one who directs or gives direction in the making of a film." They are the one who visualizes the screenplay and operates with creativity to strategically move the technical crews as well as the actors. In most cases, the director is not the writer or creator of the script but is the one who has been assigned to bring to fruition that which is in the mind of the creator. Directors are tasked with the responsibility of bringing the vision of a movie, film, play, or show to life.

> Those who possess the Gift of Administration are not the writers of the script...God is. The script for any given kingdom assignment has already been written, and the Lord calls for the administrative gifting to execute His vision and carry out that which is on His mind.

As with a secular director, one who houses the Gift of Administration has the ability, through the power of the Holy Spirit, to:

- Receive with understanding the revelation of the vision through communication with the Captain.
- Strategically develop a plan of action for the vision, anticipating any hiccups which may occur, while being willing to change course if necessary.
- Execute the plan which will give life to the vision.

Understanding the role of the helmsman, pilot, and director gives us greater clarity into the operation of the Gift of Administration. Anyone operating as a Secular Administrator may have the training, skills, or talent to do so. They are trained in handling projects and tasks; and in some cases, people. They are trained in problem-solving techniques and conceptual skills. The Gift of Administration offers grace and empowers people by the Holy Spirit to do just as Secular Administrators. However, there is spiritual revelation and insight given where there is no "cookie-cutter plan" to each circumstance, but specific instruction is given out of the mind of God. Much like the gift of the "Word of Wisdom."

There are many counselors in the world. Guidance counselors, spiritual counselors, Christian counselors, pastoral counselors, etc., and they may all do well in offering good, sound advice as they have been trained. When a counselor has the spiritual gift of the word of wisdom, they are given God's word on any given situation. Two people may have the exact same problem occurring in their life and based on training, a counselor may give them each the same resolution. With the gift of the word of wisdom, a counselor will hear from the Holy Spirit and give instruction as the Holy Spirit directs them. Though the problems may be the same, the resolution may be different.

We must understand that spiritual gifts are given by the Holy Spirit. Can one without the Holy Spirit prophesy? Can one without the Holy Spirit give the word of wisdom, the word of knowledge, or interpret tongues? One with administrative training may be able to perform certain administrative functions but they will not be able to execute with the same depth of revelation and accuracy as one with the Gift of Administration.

1 Corinthians 12 explains that the gifts of the Spirit are the manifestation of the Spirit and have been given to every believer for the profit, advancement, and benefit of the Body of Christ. We must take note that talents with similar functions may be learned and executed by skilled people who have absolutely no relationship with Christ at all. These talents include hospitality, service, teaching, giving, exhortation, leading, and of course, administration.

Let's look at teachers for instance. Secular teachers can be taught and given strategies for teaching. However, teaching as a spiritual gift is not taught, and there is no secular training that takes place to acquire the needed skills. The gift of teaching is an endowment of grace by the Holy Spirit and comes with a supernatural impartation of revelation and knowledge. Just to be clear, although spiritual gifts are not taught, they must yet be discovered by the believer. Undiscovered gifts can lie dormant in the believer. Once a gift is discovered, it must then be developed. Developing the gift of teaching does not give one the skillsets needed to teach, but enhances and improves on the gift that is already there. The same is with the Gift of Administration. There are those who are talented in areas of administration…good managers who are highly organized and excellent communicators. While Secular Administrators have a place in our society, those with the Gift of Administration are most needed as they have the supernatural ability of grace that allows one to properly govern in the Kingdom of God and in the world. The Gift of Administration does not depend on one's know-how or education, but rather the power that has been vested in them by the Holy Spirit Himself.

In **Mark Chapter 6**, we can see Jesus' Gift of Administration in operation. Let's examine *the gift* versus *the talent*. After a time of ministry, healing the sick, preaching the gospel, and casting out demons, the apostles return to Jesus. Understanding the need to get away and rest, Jesus takes the apostles away to a deserted place to rest and be restored. The crowds followed, and Jesus received them and continued teaching and healing those in need. As the day progressed, the disciples recognized that the people were hungry. Their response to the need for those who were hungry was that they were in a deserted place; and in order for the people to be fed, they needed to be sent away to the surrounding cities where they might receive provision.

As with the apostles, an Administrator is *taught* to recognize a problem. The apostles had a response but no solution. Those with the "Gift of Administration" are solution-oriented. This gift allows them to "see the way out of no way." They are trendsetters and know how to bring the best out of every situation. Administrators can only go so far, but those with the gift operate with wings of faith, understanding that, "Nothing is impossible to those who believe."

Piggybackers

Piggybackers love to rehearse the problem as if talking about it over and over again will bring a solution. If Jimmy has just said, "There is no milk," then Mike has to do a buy-in: "Let me piggyback on what Jimmy just said and say, 'I agree, there is no milk.'" I have attended many meetings with Administrators and have heard the piggybackers reiterate a problem without a solution.

One of the disciples said to Jesus, "The hour is late so send them away to buy bread for they have nothing to eat." Jesus and the disciples had been ministering all day. Certainly, everyone already knew the hour was late and everyone already knew there was nothing to eat. Tell me something I don't know.

Murmurers and Complainers

Limited Vision: Jesus' response when the disciples suggested He send the crowds away was not to send them away, but to take care of them and feed them. Their response was, "But we have only… this is all we have!" The apostles had been on many ministry journeys with Jesus. With Him…they worked miracles. Without Him…they worked miracles. The disciples laid hands on the sick, and they recovered. They cast out demons. They operated as *miracle evangelists*—but they could not see how Jesus could use them to feed so many. What were they missing? Were they too tired from a day's ministry to comprehend the fact that they could provide increase when increase was needed? If Jesus gave them the command to feed the people, surely, He knew they had the capacity to do so. Why now the limited vision?

While there may be many solutions, there's only one that is "the" solution, and this comes through the Gift of Administration, empowered by the Holy Spirit.

Questions for Reflection

- Who do you know that operates in this gifting?
- What are some of the things they have been able to accomplish because of their Gift of Administration?

Action Step

Think about how you can better appreciate, receive from, or operate in this gift as a result of what you have learned so far. What is one tangible step you can take today to reflect your newfound appreciation for your gifting?

ADMINISTRATION AND SERVANTHOOD

2

Jesus Knew Who He Was

In **John 13:1-17**, we find the greatest Administrator of all time…Jesus…who demonstrates the *foundation* of administration—*love*. The basis for everything Jesus did was because of His love for us. It's amazing to me that many people want to lead without love. **1 Corinthians 13** speaks to the fact that without love, we are *nothing*, and there is *no profit* to what we do. Without love…*nothing. else. matters.* The Apostle Paul declared, *"I speak the truth **in love** and lie not."* The Apostle John says that if we love God, we must love our brothers. Without love, everything we do is void. I believe that most people *want* to truly love, and many believe that they *do* love; however, they may be challenged by the fact that they don't know *how* to love.

The perfect example for love is exemplified through the life of Jesus. During His time on earth, He found it easy to serve because of His love. I hear so many people speak of those whom they have been called to serve as those who are "irritating them" and "getting on their last nerve." We must be reminded that we have been *called* to serve. If people have become irritants and annoyances to us, then perhaps we may need to inspect our heart, check our motives, and, when necessary, redirect our focus. To sum it up...*check yourself before you wreck yourself.* (A very appropriate quote that my dear nephew shared with me.)

In **John 13:1-15**, Jesus teaches us how to serve as He washes the disciples' feet. Jesus sums up the basis of His service in the first three verses. He knew...

- *That the Father **had given all things** into His hands.*
- *He had **come from** God.*
- *He was **going to** God.*

> "Who being in the form of God, did not consider it robbery to be equal with God, but made Himself of no reputation, taking the form of a **bondservant**, and coming in the likeness of men."
> Philippians 2:6-7 (NKJV)

Jesus knew *who* He was...*whose* He was...and His *divine purpose.*

With urgency and sincerity of heart, Jesus rises from His supper and begins to demonstrate the actions of a true servant, washing the disciples' feet. Foot washing was a very menial task and reserved for the lowliest of servants. Jesus had no problem taking on servanthood to demonstrate the very essence of it because *He knew who He was*: the Savior of the world, the Christ, the King, the Ruler of heaven and earth.

Nearing the time for Jesus to go to the cross, the disciples had walked throughout this journey with Him. They had watched Lazarus being raised from the dead, saw the opening of the eyes of the man born blind, participated in the distribution of food during the feeding of 5,000, and even beheld Christ walking on water. Oh, the miracles they witnessed! During their walk with Jesus, they also observed His character and interaction with those He came in contact with. They watched how He treated everyone He encountered—but did they connect that with servanthood? Here, Jesus has a lesson on servanthood He must teach. If not now, when? Would there be another opportunity? They *watched* and *observed* Jesus…but did they *get it*?

If Jesus simply wanted to convey the "image" of a servant, He could have used a "stuntman." In the theater, stuntmen are used to do the "dirty work." They jump off of high buildings, get hit by trains, and are in car accidents. Surely, foot washing is "dirty work." Surely, a *King* would not wash feet. Why not use a double? Why not a stuntman? Jesus did not portray an "image." He demonstrated the example and true character of a servant. Too many are concerned with showmanship, and being seen or noticed, rather than servanthood…which is never about recognition, but is an act that comes from the heart. Jesus was never concerned with showmanship, but servanthood.

Jesus laid aside His garments in order to wash the feet of His disciples. His garments didn't "make" Him and laying them aside represented Jesus laying aside His title. He was a King but laid aside His title for the sake of teaching the disciples the importance of having a servant's heart. He was God but laid His deity aside to take on the form of man that He might die for the sins of the world. It was never the clothing that defined who He was, but rather the chambers of His heart. The world gets hung up on titles, designer clothing, where we live, and what we drive. In contrast, Jesus demonstrated that *titles* and *material things* were not at the top of His agenda…*servanthood* was.

Jesus took a towel and girded Himself to wash the disciples' feet. Towels are used to clean, wash dishes, or dust tables. Towels are used in restaurants to bus tables and to keep things neat and clean. It was the servant's responsibility to take a towel and wash the feet of kings and guests who would enter the home after walking through the dust and dirt of the streets. But Jesus took a towel. Towels are also used for covering the body when one gets out of a swimming pool or shower. Jesus' use of the towel further exemplified His covering of His people by His blood. Love covers a multitude of sin, and Jesus took away our sin with the covering of His blood.

Jesus focused himself on the task at hand. He did not focus on the fact that He was washing the disciples' feet but that this would be His last opportunity to show them what true servanthood looks like. Perhaps they didn't get it in previous attempts or previous conversations they may have had. Could it be possible that they got so caught up in the glory of casting out devils, healing the sick, prophesying, preaching, and hanging out with Jesus that they missed who He was—a *servant, who took a towel*?

> "...the Son of Man did not come to be served, but to serve, and to give His life a ransom for many."
> **Matthew 20:28 (NKJV)**

Peter's response to Jesus washing the disciples' feet was, "You shall never wash my feet." Peter knew Jesus was Lord and Savior, and further recognized that foot washing was a servant's responsibility. Peter was caught up in an outward expression that did not initiate from the heart. Jesus was more concerned about the heart and helping us to understand that the concept of servanthood is not just an external expression, but an expression of the heart. Anything one does which does not initiate from the heart results in *showmanship*, not *servanthood*.

Questions for Reflection

- We see Jesus taking two fish and five loaves and feeding at least 5,000 people. What do you most appreciate about Jesus in His role as an Administrator?
- Why does humility play a key factor in effectively operating in this role?
- Why is it important to the Body of Christ, as a whole, that Jesus demonstrated servanthood by washing His disciples' feet? Please explain in detail.

Action Step

Find a way to step outside of your comfort zone and "take a towel" to serve this week. Here are some ideas:

- Volunteer at a food bank or soup kitchen.
- Call your local nursing home and ask if they have residents who don't receive visitors. (I guarantee that they do.) Spend some time reading to them, listening to them, or just holding their hand and praying with them.
- Take a meal to a family in your church. Pray about it, and ask the Lord to show you who may be in need of some "comfort food" this week.
- Send the single mother and her child/children to the movies.
- Purchase a Starbucks gift card for your church administrator.

3

Jesus Knew Whose He Was

"But as many as received him, to them gave He power to become the sons of God, even to them that believe on his name."
JOHN 1:12 *(KJV)*

Jesus had a relationship and a sense of belonging. **Luke 3:22** says that when Jesus was baptized, the voice from heaven affirmed him and confirmed who He was as the beloved Son of God. He knew Sonship and did not operate out of an "orphan spirit." An orphan spirit typifies characteristics of abandonment, alienation, isolation, jealousy, and competition. In addition, people-pleasers and those with feelings of low self-worth and low self-esteem may also exhibit behaviors of one who has succumbed to an orphan spirit. Those bearing such a spirit accept labels that others put upon them as their means of identity because they have no other sense of belonging.

Who we belong to is a direct correlation with our identity; and when we are insecure in whom we belong, we will try to identify with others. The woman at the well had no sense of belonging so she went from man to man, looking for a husband…someone to affirm her and make her feel good about herself. Perhaps she was looking for a "father" image to identify with. Someone to connect with as family.

We have Sonship! We are not orphans, as we have been adopted into the Body of Christ. We don't have to look for someone to belong to. We have a loving Heavenly Father and belong to a family of faith!

It is through the blood of Jesus that every born-again believer has been connected. In **Galatians 6:10**, when the Apostle Paul addressed the churches in Galatia, he said, *"Therefore, as we have opportunity, let us do good to all, especially to those who are of the household of faith."*

What a tremendous blessing to belong to the household of faith and have kinship in the Body of Christ through the blood of Jesus. The family of faith loves at all times, even though we know one another's strengths, weaknesses, failures, and mess-ups. We also know character, when we are right and when we are wrong, and are commanded to still love no matter what. Although we have different personalities and different levels of natural and spiritual maturity, we are still of the same family. We do not all think the same or understand the same way.

Some of us are emotional, while others are fearful. There are those who are bold…while others are more sensitive. Some of us have become hardened and are guarded with our emotions…and some people are an open book.

Some understand well…and some have very little understanding. There are those who seek to be *understood*…while others seek to *understand*. Some of us have to always be right…and some have learned how to lay down our ego for the sake of peace.

The church is full of gossipers and slanderers…and also those who will shut it down. There are those of us who are very needy…

and some of us who are too independent. Whatever category we fall into, we recognize one thing: **not one of us is perfect. No one has "arrived."** Yet we are still family.

Let's look at the lives of those who walked closest to Jesus… His disciples.

- Peter was in Jesus' inner circle and was one of His closest friends. Enthusiastic Peter was honest, frank, forthright, and outspoken, and never held back that which was on his mind. Peter walked closely with Jesus, yet he had some anger issues. He could curse like a sailor and would cut you in a heartbeat, as he demonstrated when he cut off the ear of the soldier who came to apprehend Jesus. Nevertheless, Peter was still a part of the family of faith.

- James and John were also a part of Jesus' inner circle. They operated out of their emotions and didn't know how to handle rejection. When Jesus was not received in the Samaritan village as they thought He should have been, they wanted to call down fire from heaven on those who rejected them. **(Luke 9:51-54)** Jesus had to remind them that they were not of the right spirit. They loved Jesus, but they had rejection issues they had to deal with.

There was a report issued in 2001 by the Surgeon General of the United States, stating that rejection was a greater contributor for adolescent violence than drugs, poverty, or gang membership. If rejection is not properly handled, it can result in aggressive behaviors and outbursts of anger.

They also dealt with a sense of entitlement. In **Mark 10:35**, they said to Jesus, *"Teacher, we want You to do for us whatever we ask."* How funny…and yet how *dare* they! They had the audacity to think that Jesus needed to do a special favor for them. Entitlement! It is sad to think how so many people believe that God "owes" them. The reality is that He *owes* us nothing but *gives* us everything. And not only did James and John deal with feelings of rejection and the attitude of entitlement, they were also position-seekers. *"Jesus, we want to sit with You in Your glory. Let one of us sit on Your right hand and the other on Your left."* Matthew says the mother of James and John went with them to Jesus. Could it be that James and John were influenced by their mother? Nonetheless, they were a part of the family of faith.

- The Apostle John, (the very same John who had the rejection issues, the entitlement problem, and that pesky position-seeking attitude) in writing the Book of John, believed he had a "heads up" on everyone else and called himself "the disciple whom Jesus loved." The truth of the matter is that he was—and *so were all of the others*. We are all the ones "whom Jesus loves," none being left out, and none insignificant. My parents had seven children, and we were all made to believe we were my mother's favorite. She loved us all and made each one of us feel special. That is what love is like in the family of faith. Jesus loves us all and to Him, we are all special. There is never a need to put others down to make ourselves look better. We are all loved, and we are all special.

- Judas, the betrayer of Jesus, was a backstabber. He would smile to your face, speak kind words, hug, and kiss you outwardly…but inwardly, he was a betrayer. Jesus knew exactly who Judas was and exactly how to deal with him. I'm sure Judas would have wanted to be part of Jesus' inner circle but Jesus, in His infinite wisdom, knew how to keep him at bay. Yet Judas was still a part of the family of faith. Think it not strange that there are Judases in our lives. We just need to know how to deal with them.

Jesus, the greatest Administrator ever, loved His disciples even with their issues. He taught them what servanthood was and knew exactly how to deal with each one's personality and character. He never disowned any of them but continued to love them. He never kicked them to the curb but continued to teach them as he recognized the strengths and weaknesses in each. There is a saying that the Lord gave to me many years ago: *"When you know what a person is like, you deal with them accordingly."* Jesus was an expert at dealing with people right where they are. Those with the Gift of Administration will have to ask, like Solomon did, *"Lord, give me wisdom to move in and out among this so great of people."*

As the family of faith, we must scrutinize people before including them in our social settings and certainly our inner circles. There are times when people act out publicly, and we need to "put them on blast." Look at how Jesus handled the Pharisees. When they challenged Him openly, He rebuked them openly. Then there are times when we need to speak to people privately. We do not need to put everyone's mistakes on blast. **1 Peter 4:8** says love covers a multitude of sins. People with administrative giftings know how and when to cover, and how and when to openly rebuke.

In the family of faith, there are always those that we love who are whisperers and gossipers. There are always those who are looking for someone to dump on—and we must remind them we are not the trash. When we get tired of hearing the negative murmuring and complaining, we may need to consider putting those we love on mute, much like we silence our phone when we need a moment's peace. Jesus knew who He was, and He knew when He had to silence those who were not going in the same direction that He was traveling.

Questions for Reflection

- What are some things that we use to "affirm" ourselves when we don't get what we need from our family?
- Have you ever been betrayed by someone close to you? How did you deal with the fallout? Have you been able to forgive the person? What did that look like?

Action Step

Spend some time this week studying the stories of Peter, James, John, and Judas. How were they alike? How were they different? If this story were playing out today on social media, how do you think it would look?

Jesus Knew His Purpose

The late Dr. Myles Munroe once said, *"Where purpose is not known, abuse is inevitable."* It's difficult to know our purpose and destiny if we don't know who we *are* or who we *belong to*. **Isaiah 46:10** says God has already declared our end from the beginning and has placed oil on the inside of us to accomplish and fulfill our purpose.

In **1 Corinthians 15:8**, the Apostle Paul considers himself "as one born out of due time." Paul did not have the opportunity that the other apostles had to walk with Jesus throughout the years of His ministry. Paul was not a part of Jesus' inner circle. He did not see Him perform miracles nor did he receive a direct impartation from Jesus' teachings. He did not receive the benefits of the incubation or gestation periods with Christ. Paul's call and ministry were birthed out of an encounter with the Lord. As Paul—then known as Saul—was going about his business, persecuting Christians, he had an encounter with Jesus that transformed his life and launched him into ministry.

> "Then Saul, still breathing threats and murder against the disciples of the Lord, went to the high priest and asked letters from him to the synagogues of Damascus, so that if he found any who were of the Way, whether men or women, he might bring them bound to Jerusalem.
>
> As he journeyed, he came near Damascus, and suddenly a light shone around him from heaven. Then he fell to the ground, and heard a voice saying to him, 'Saul, Saul, why are you persecuting Me?'
>
> And he said, 'Who are You, Lord?'
>
> Then the Lord said, 'I am Jesus, whom you are persecuting. It is hard for you to kick against the goads.'
>
> So he, trembling and astonished, said, 'Lord, what do You want me to do?'
>
> Then the Lord said to him, 'Arise and go into the city, and you will be told what you must do.'
>
> And the men who journeyed with him stood speechless, hearing a voice but seeing no one. Then Saul arose from the ground, and when his eyes were opened, he saw no one. But they led him by the hand and brought him into Damascus. And he was three days without sight, and neither ate nor drank."
>
> **Acts 9: 1-9 (NKJV)**

I want to encourage those of you who feel as though you have had a late start, may have lacked the same training or opportunities as others, and who feel as though you don't fit in anywhere because you are too young or too old.

> *Don't negate or abort your ministry...because the deal is still on and the call upon your life is still in effect. Your purpose must be fulfilled. God called you and still has need of you.*

Even though you feel as though you should be further along in life, you must continue to declare that you are here "for such a time as this," and you will fulfill every assignment the Lord has given to you.

Apostle Paul considered himself the "least of the apostles" and not worthy of the title. He did not fall victim to the "Black Sheep" syndrome, for he knew who he was. Sometimes, I hear people refer to themselves as the "black sheep" of their family. What they are saying is they feel as though they do not belong or fit in because they are different. They feel left out, an outcast, or left behind. Those who have the "Black Sheep" syndrome often feel victimized and carry a "woe is me" attitude. Victimized people who have never been healed will rarely accept responsibility for their actions and will often play the blame game.

> *There are no "black sheep" in the Kingdom of God...so rise up and be the victor that you are, and declare by the grace of God, "I am what I am!"*

Paul understood how one's past could very easily lead to feelings of unimportance, as he started out as an enemy and adversary of the church. Paul, however, never allowed the shame and guilt of the past to prevent him from possessing his future. Paul owned it! *Never allow your disappointments and failures of the past to negate your future.* God uses who we are: our character, failures, griefs, opposition, experiences, and the obstacles in our lives.

Paul traveled more and experienced more grief and opposition than any of the other apostles…yet, he wrote more New Testament epistles and founded more churches than any of the other apostles!

If we know that we are people of purpose, we do what we must do. Not because of a title, but because it is who we are. We just do it! *What* you are is *who* you are, and because of *who you are*, you *produce*. Jesus said in **John 15:16**, *"You did not choose Me, but I chose you and ordained you that you should go and bring forth fruit, and that your fruit should remain."*

> *"If a person is who he ought to be, he will do what he ought to do"*

Many times throughout life's challenges, we may find ourselves saying, "I didn't choose this" or "I didn't sign up for that," referring to the conditions of life or ministry. While we recognize it is not our choice to experience the unpleasant times in life, we do understand that "all things will work together for our good." In the process of all things working out, God still uses us, because He knew from the foundation of the world what our "this" and "that" in life would be. He also knows the timing of every challenge; and yet, He *still* chose us. We are challenged when we say life is too difficult so we cannot do what God called us to do. The Lord gives us grace to accomplish everything He has assigned to our hands.

He chose us to bear and bring forth fruit. There will be differences in our fruit, because there are differences in us as trees! There are differences in our assignments as well as differences in our calls. There are differences in our ministries and differences in how we execute our gifting. We are all unique. We have *no one* and *nothing* to compare ourselves to. We are to be valued as God has called us. Not every Administrator is the same. Our character is different, our lifestyles are different, our calling is different, and our mode of execution is different.

Apostle Paul was uniquely different from Apostle Peter, and Apostle Peter from Apostle John. We are different and must learn to appreciate ourselves as well as appreciate the differences in others. As diverse as we are, we will all produce fruit…and Jesus says our fruit will remain. As long as we stay connected to the vine (Jesus), we will not have to worry about our fruit spoiling, falling to the ground before its time, or never ripening.

Questions for Reflection

- The Apostle Paul did not have the opportunity to walk and talk with Jesus as the other disciples did; and yet, he was able to serve Him faithfully from the time of his conversion until the end of his life. What circumstances in your life have you thought may be "holding you back" from living out the purpose that God has called you to?

- What are some practical steps that you can take to throw off the past and move forward into His will for your life?

Action Step

Read the words of Paul in the New Testament. Notice how he chose to move forward in his calling, throwing off his past, and refusing to let it affect his future.

ADMINISTRATION AND THE OIL OF ANOINTING

5

Oil for Your Purpose

In **Acts 19**, we see that "unusual" or "special" miracles were wrought by the hands of Apostle Paul. Paul operated in an Authentic Anointing, as he was authenticated as a delegated authority to operate in miracles, signs, and wonders. This authentication came from the Lord Jesus, who bore witness to his testimony and granted signs and wonders to be done by his hands. To walk in *Authentic Authority*, one must possess *Authentic Anointing*. You have been endowed with the authenticity of the anointing.

> "The Spirit of the Lord is upon me, because He has **anointed** Me to preach the gospel to the poor; He sent Me to heal the brokenhearted, to proclaim liberty to the captives and recovery of sight to the blind, to set at liberty those who are oppressed; to proclaim the acceptable year of the Lord…"
> **Luke 4:18-19 (NKJV)**

When Jesus came to Nazareth, He went into the synagogue on the Sabbath. When they handed Him the Book of Isaiah, He began to read the prophecy from **Isaiah 61:1** and came into agreement with what the Word of God said about Him and the anointing that was upon His life.

What is this anointing? Let's look at both the Hebrew and Greek forms of this word.

In the Old Testament, the Hebrew word for anointing is ***shemen***. Shemen means "fat, fatness, or oil." We find this word in **Isaiah 10:27**, where the Scripture says, *"It shall come to pass in that day that his burden will be taken away from your shoulder, and his yoke from your neck, and the yoke will be destroyed because of the anointing oil."* The yoke is destroyed because of the fatness and oil of the anointing.

Merriam Webster Online gives us thorough definitions for *yoke*. I will choose to use five of these:

- A wooden bar or frame by which two draft animals (such as oxen) are joined at the heads or necks for the purpose of working together.
- An arched device formerly laid on the neck of a defeated person.
- A frame fitted to a person's shoulders to carry a load in two equal portions.
- An oppressive agency.
- Servitude and bondage.

From these definitions, we learn that oxen were yoked together at the neck to perform labor, allowing difficult tasks to be made easy. In the natural, oxen were also yoked, usually the younger with the older, for training purposes. Spiritual yokes were also placed on people to identify one's defeat and further represent a load too heavy to carry, as well as a weight of oppression and bondage. *"Therefore, if the Son makes you free, you shall be free indeed."* **John 8:36**. As those who are no longer bound, we must know, it is not our portion to be under bondage or oppression. One must be careful of becoming unequally yoked, as unequally yoked oxen can work against one another rather than working together.

Destroying the Yoke of Bondage

A metaphor of the anointing or fatness which destroys the yoke can be viewed as oxen which are being trained and having a yoke placed about them. As they continue to eat and grow, they will eventually break the yoke, thus terminating its restraint and bondage. This same use applies to those who are under heavy oppression, weights, or pressure as well as those who are in bondage and who have been labeled defeated. I implore you to continue to eat the Word, feast in prayer, and grow fat in Christ, remembering that He always causes us to triumph. As you grow fat, you will begin to see yokes of bondage in your life destroyed, causing you to become free to be who God has called you to be. There are weights of oppression operating in churches with religious spirits at the helm. Grow fat, and watch these oppressions be destroyed!

As those with the Gift of Administration, we must also understand it is not for us to put others under the yokes of bondage or yokes of oppression. Those with the Gift of Administration must be ever so careful to not set plumb lines and bars, expecting others to live up to their standard. We have the anointing to identify bondage and to break it, not to place it upon others. We are free and know what it took for us to get free. Without grace, those with the Gift of Administration can put oppression on others, expecting them to live up to standards they do not have the grace or capacity for.

Questions for Reflection

- Have you come into agreement with what God says about you and your anointing?
- Have you ever felt "unequally yoked?" What was the situation, and how were you able to resolve it?

Action Step

Spend some time in prayer this week, asking the Lord to show you areas of your life where you may need to break the yoke of bondage.

6

Authentic Anointing vs. Counterfeit Anointing

The Greek word for anointing is ***chrisma***, found in the New Testament, Scriptures **1 John 2:20** and **27**.

> *"But you have an **anointing** from the Holy One." "But the **anointing** which you have received from Him abides in you."*

This word "chrisma" is not to be confused with "charisma," the word for "gifts." *Charisma* may also be viewed as "a compelling charm or personality which influential people possess." The Greek word for anointing, *chrisma*, is an unguent and ointment. It means "to smear, spread, coat, cover, or rub." Chrisma is an endowment of the Holy Spirit and is the power and ability granted by God to perform a given assignment.

A few noteworthy thoughts regarding the anointing:

- The anointing **cannot be bought**.

- The anointing is **not attained by social status, race, or gender.**
- The anointing is **increased as we decrease.**
- The anointing is **increased as we grow fat and come into the knowledge of the truth.**
- The anointing is **not for everyone.** It is only for believers as it is because of Jesus Christ, "Christos," the Anointed One, that the anointing lives on the inside of us…thus empowering us to do greater works than Jesus did. The more you pour out your oil, the more your oil will increase.
- The anointing **is contagious.**

In **Acts 19:11**, Paul finds himself in the presence of those who recognize that there is something different about him. People were healed and demons were cast out when he spoke, laid hands, and handkerchiefs were sent from his body. Those who served under a false authority wanted what Paul had. Whenever we operate in the Authentic Anointing, the world will behold the true miracles of heaven and desire what we have. They will know that Jesus is real and that He is the one, the only, true, and Living God!

Paraclete or Parakeet?

The itinerant or "vagabond" Jews mentioned in **Acts 19** performed exorcisms as a profession and would go from city to city, pretending to cure with charms and spells, those who were considered demon-possessed. They were magicians, using chants and magical spells out of a Counterfeit Anointing. What gives us the authenticity is our Paraclete—the Holy Ghost who is our Helper.

Philip the Evangelist is another example of one who operated out of the Authentic Anointing. As an evangelist with oil, Philip was authenticated as a delegated authority to operate in miracles, signs, wonders, and deliverances. *People with oil don't have to fake it.* Many are still trying to figure out their oil, and one thing is for certain—*when you tap into the authentic oil that you house, you will never again settle for the counterfeit.* As Philip operates in the authentic oil, we also see the counterfeit in action.

Watch Out for the Copycats

In **Acts 8**, we see Philip possessing an Authentic Anointing and Simon the Sorcerer wanting what he has. *When you have authentic oil, you must know there will always be copycats.* Philip's anointing was birthed out of an authentic relationship with Christ. Simon wanted the oil without relationship. He wanted the oil without the struggle, the ostracizing, the beatings, the shaking, and the crushing rejection. Simon practiced sorcery, and he boasted among the people that he was someone great, so much so that the people were impressed and began to say of him, "This man is the great power of God." Philip's true anointing, like that which Simon desperately wanted, was not to impress people but rather to exalt the living God. Simon wanted the oil Philip and the apostles possessed, and he was willing to pay a monetary price for it. To his dismay, he found the anointing could not be bought!

The Counterfeit Anointing operates out of a Parakeet spirit. The parakeet is a bird from the parrot family that can imitate human speech, learning up to one hundred words or more. The Parakeet spirit copies, mimics, and imitates that which the Paraclete does. And so it is with the Mockingbird spirit. Mockingbirds are best known for mimicking the songs of other birds as well as the sounds of amphibians and insects. These birds sing loudly and in rapid succession. As with the parakeet, the mockingbird has no originality of speech, but copies and mimics the other birds.

We are authentic and must maintain our authenticity. We do

not copy. We do not say what "they" say—we say what *God* says. The itinerant Jewish exorcists, the seven sons of Sceva, and Simon the Sorcerer all operated out of a "Parakeet and Mockingbird" spirit. They had no true power but wanted to be seen and exalted among men whom they could impress. The anointing of Paul and Philip produced great results because it was of authentic origin. The others were impersonators, impressionists, and copycats who wanted a form of godliness but denied the power thereof.

Speak with Power

I am concerned that the Church has begun to operate out of these Parakeet and Mockingbird spirits. How so? How could this be with the Church? We have allowed words and actions of men to "creep in unaware." **(Jude 4) Matthew 13:25** says, *"While men slept, his enemy came in and sowed tares among the wheat and went his way."* The Gnostic and New Age religions of the world have established a "speak it into the atmosphere" theory. They believe, if you "speak it" to the universe then "it" will come back to you." If you put "it" out there into the elements, the elements will work for you.

God does not speak **into** the atmosphere; He speaks **to it,** specifically to **things**, with the voice of command. When God speaks, He speaks to both animate and inanimate objects. When God speaks, His words are targeted, as with a laser beam. **Isaiah 55:11** says, *"So shall My word be that goeth forth out of My mouth, it shall not return unto Me void, but shall accomplish that which I please and it shall prosper in the **thing** whereto I sent it."*

In **Genesis 1:1-3**, God spoke and said, *"Let 'there' be light."* Where is there? In the *earth*! It was the earth that was without form and void. So God spoke into the *earth* realm and commanded that light be "there" in the earth. Further, in **Mark 11:23**, Jesus says, *"For assuredly I say to you, whoever says to this mountain, 'Be removed and be cast into the sea,' and does not doubt in his heart..."* If you speak to this mountain...Jesus encourages us to speak to the mountains...not into the atmosphere. He tells us not to just *speak* to the mountain but to give it *direction*, and tell it where to *go*. It is time we tell some obstacles, demons, and even some people, where to go. Be thou cast into the sea.

In **Ezekiel 37: 4-6**, Ezekiel was charged to prophesy to the dry bones and then to prophesy to the Breath of Life. *"Then he said to me, "***Speak** *a prophetic message to these bones and say, 'Dry bones, listen to the word of the Lord! This is what the Sovereign Lord says: Look! I am going to put breath into you and make you live again!"*

Isaiah 43:5-6 says, *"Fear not, for I am with thee; I will bring thy seed from the east, and gather thee from the west; I will **say** to the north "Give up" and to the south "Keep not back" bring my sons from far, and my daughters from the ends of the earth."* God declares He will speak to the directions of North and South.

Learning to Echo Heaven

Words spoken into the atmosphere wander aimlessly, without direction or purpose. A rocket ship, after being programmed, will be launched into orbit and sent to its destination. When it is launched, it will not wander aimlessly in the atmosphere; but rather, will penetrate the atmosphere to arrive at its programmed destination. The words that God speaks are more powerful than any rocket ship and have a programmed destination.

Our words as well are spoken with power and authority and will penetrate the atmosphere and find the thing to where they have been sent. The words of the authentically anointed are words of power and authority and cause life and death to take place. We must learn to echo heaven. We say what God says, and we do as

God does. Let Thy kingdom come, and Thy will be done on earth as it is in heaven. What are you saying in heaven, God? Let me say what you say on earth. Those with the Gift of Administration truly walk in the anointing to do what they do. They have the authentic authority to say what God says and release heaven's desire on earth. They will lock into the anointing which destroys yokes and are poised and purposed to set the oppressed free. One with the Gift of Administration finds it difficult to watch others performing or living beneath their God-given ability and through the grace given to them, they have been given full authority to walk alongside one in bondage, raising them up to their place of victory.

Questions for Reflection

- Think about the words that you speak. Do you speak with purpose and direction? Power and authority? Do your words "echo heaven" or "just echo?"

- Have you ever known someone who operated out of a Parakeet spirit? Were their words easily discernable as false, or were others led astray by their flowery, fake prose?

Action Step

Think of someone you know who operates out of an Authentic Anointing. What qualities or characteristics do you see in them that bear out their anointing? Sit at their feet (either literally or figuratively) for an hour this week and just listen.

Take time this week to practice echoing heaven and say what God says. Find a Scripture that speaks to what God says about you, and begin to declare it daily.

7

Owning Your Oil

In **2 Kings 4:1-7**, we find the story of the widow woman, the wife of one who served under Elisha the prophet. The widow goes to Elisha with a situation, believing that he, being a prophet, could help solve it. She said, *"My husband, your servant, is dead, and we are broke. We are out of money and loaded in debt which we are unable to pay. Now, the creditors have come to take my sons as indentured servants to pay the debt."* The widow woman had been dealing with this situation for so long, trying to make ends meet, that she had now run out of time. They were coming to take her sons. She was desperate and cried out, "Elisha! Help me!"

Looking Within

Elisha did not take it upon himself to work a miracle for her. In fact, he did not even release the Word of the Lord. Elisha did not solve her problem but caused her to look within her means and take inventory of what she possessed. The answer to what she needed did not rest with *Elisha* but rested inside of *her*. He caused her to look at what she possessed to solve her problem. Elijah operated with the Gift of Administration. He caused the woman to see what she otherwise could not.

> What's your gift, talent, or passion? Could it be that **the very thing you believe is going to take you out is that which will take you up?** Could it be that the very thing that is pulling **on you** is trying to pull something **out of you**? You have the oil to bring yourself out of this situation!

Do You Understand?

Although her husband was a prophet, one has to wonder if she understood the oil. If you do not *understand* the oil, you cannot *value* the oil. The woman went to the right person—Elisha the prophet. She could have gone to her negative, compromising, arrogant friends; but instead, she went to the man of God. Something miraculous happens when you come in contact with a true man or woman of God. They will cause the oil on the inside of you to leap, and you will be challenged to take inventory of what is in your house…and *own it.*

The prophet of God challenged the widow woman to look within herself and call forth her oil, for the oil she had was valuable. Her faith was activated as she followed Elisha's instructions and borrowed vessels from her neighbors. Her oil flowed continuously, because she was obedient and followed the prophets' orders. The more she poured out, the more the vessels were supernaturally filled. She poured until there were no more vessels to fill. The oil she possessed was so valuable that she lived off the residue of it for the rest of her life. Remember…you are a distribution center, and you carry an *Authentic Anointing*. Your oil is valuable and is not for you only, but for you to pour out into others.

As one with the Gift of Administration, you can never hold back your anointing…which means there is *no room* for second guessing yourself. You are anointed and you see what you see, know what you know, and must move as you have been directed to do so. You are an anointing stirrer. When people come in contact with *you*, they see what God sees about *them*. Their anointing is stirred and their babies leap. There is movement and motion in the kingdom…because they have come into the *knowledge of the truth* about what they possess.

You as one housing the Gift of Administration recognize their importance in the kingdom and have set them in motion to fulfill their assignment.

Questions for Reflection

- What situation are you facing right now that you need the oil of the Lord to overcome?

Action Step

It's time to "take inventory." What talents and gifts do you possess that have the power to bring you out of your current situation? Write them down as affirmations, one to a note card, and place them where you will see them daily. Carry some in your purse or pocket. Bring them out when you feel overwhelmed and need to call on the Lord.

8

Using Your Oil

We have established that God speaks to things. His Word does not wander and linger in the atmosphere. If His Words were to linger in the atmosphere, Satan would have a play day with them. God's Words are directed, and so must our words be. We are the church, and we serve the God who created the universe, the elements, and the atmosphere. We operate with an Authentic Anointing, and we don't speak anything into the atmosphere with an expectation of it fulfilling a prayer or need for us. We are people of power and authority who use their oil to set and control atmospheres.

Setting the Atmosphere

Psalm 22:3 says, *"But You are holy, enthroned in the praises of Israel."* The Lord inhabits, abides, and dwells in the praises of His people. We set the atmosphere through our praise and worship. When the praises go up, the Blessor Himself comes down and abides among us. As we sing, pray, praise, and worship, we set the atmosphere for the presence of the Lord.

> Praise and worship should never be done to entertain—we have concerts for that purpose. Praise and worship have been ordained by heaven to usher in the presence of God; to set the atmosphere for a movement of the Holy Spirit where healing and deliverance can take place.

On a personal note, I no longer desire to be a part of a "church" service where the presence of God is not welcomed or received. I do not desire to be entertained. I often tell the Lord, "If you are not going to be there, let me know, and I won't go either!" My prayer is, "Lord, may we return to the heart of worship, where we desire the Blessor and are not running after the blessings. When we have the Blessor, we have everything. The Blessor is permanent and eternal, whereas the blessings are only temporal."

> *"Now it happened on a certain day as He was teaching, that there were Pharisees and teachers of the law sitting by, who had come out of every town of Galilee, Judea and Jerusalem. And the power of the Lord was present to heal them."*
> **Luke 5:17 (NKJV)**

The atmosphere was set, charged with the power of God, and conducive for Him to move. But we have Pharisees sitting by. Were they judging, fault finding, or fact finding? They were sitting by, being spectators rather than participants. Participants engage and receive. We must set the atmosphere in our churches if we have an expectation for God to truly "show up and show out."

Beware of the Jezebel Spirit

Not only do we *set* the atmosphere, but we also *control* it. One must discern an atmosphere and the spirits or spiritual heaviness therein. People will often come into our midst and bring their heaviness, negativity, doubt, and double-mindedness with them. It is up to us to shift that atmosphere. What I am finding out is that when we surround ourselves with people who carry "Jezebel spirits" (spirits of disbelief, spirits of jealousy, and rage), that if their spirit is stronger than ours, they can overpower us and before long we will think or act like them.

Does this sound familiar? You go into a store to make a purchase. You have just gotten out of your car after listening to amazing worship music, and you are set for the day. After you finish shopping, you proceed to the check-out counter. The cashier has an attitude and is angry and frustrated with the last customer…and now they have an attitude with you. You try to shift the atmosphere and greet the cashier, because they have yet to say hello. At this point, they answer you with a very sharp "Hello," and are now almost throwing your items that they have just rung up. Before you know it, you have an attitude towards them. The angry and frustrated spirit has been jumped on to you.

Ever consider how happy and excited you are about your church and how much you love to worship and serve? And then that one disgruntled member who has been in the same position or failed position forever wants to hang out and "love on you." Before long, this person begins to subtly mention their dislikes and disapproval of how things are run at church, and before you know it you find that your joy has been stolen, and the enjoyment to serve is no longer there.

We are a ministry who "enters into His gates with thanksgiving and into His courts with praise." Although not required, we typically stand during praise worship and allow the Lord to have His way. Oh, what a beautiful presence and time of fellowship we have with Him. On the occasions when we have a special service and many visitors are present, we find those who do not come with a spirit of *"expectation"*, but rather a spirit of *"spectation."* We can sense the difference in the atmosphere. I have found that at times, some of our members will allow the presence of people and the spirit they carry to dominate the atmosphere. I frequently remind them that this is *our* house, and in our house, we *do what we do*. We are never to allow another spirit to come in and rest upon our services. Our service is committed to the Lord, and we must take control of the atmosphere, shifting it to where the Spirit of the Lord has complete control.

This is what the Scripture speaks about in **1 Corinthians 15:33**, when Paul tells us that *"Evil company corrupts good behavior."* There is something that takes place in the spirit realm when a good person hangs out with one who is spiritually unstable. This imbalance can cause us to falter. We must continue to grow in the Word so that we are able to recognize these spirits as they manifest. If we are able to do so, we will be able to control and shift the atmosphere. We have not been called to "agree with foolishness," but rather to bring those types of atmospheres and behaviors under submission to the Holy Spirit.

Questions for Reflection

- When we spend time with someone who is "spiritually unstable," their attitude can quickly affect us. We need to remove ourselves from the situation but continue to pray for them. Is there (or has there been) someone in your life who is affecting your walk because of their attitude? How do you/did you handle them?

- Sometimes, we encounter the Jezebel spirit…and sometimes, we *are* the Jezebel spirit. What things in your life can cause you to affect those around you with your attitude…and what can you do right now to change that?

Action Step

Think of a situation in your life that is causing you to "agree with foolishness." Spend some focused time in prayer over the next few days, asking the Lord to open your eyes and change your attitude regarding the situation. And remember—we may not be able to change the situation—but with the Lord's help, we can change how we respond or react to it.

ADMINISTRATION AND CHARACTER

9

Think It and Do It

We are *authentic* and we are *anointed*. Those housing the Gift of Administration recognize that greatness and success is *everyone's* portion. Behind the most successful businesses, corporations, families, athletes, authors, entrepreneurs, employees, etc. lies a spirit of determination. Determined people never give up. Determined people are strong-minded people. They are resolute, focused, and unwavering. Most of us have come this far by faith… because we have determined to persevere and *never give up*.

As a Man Thinks, So Is He

It has been said that we become a product of our environment. When babies are born, they have no particular way of thinking. Every child will pick up traits and personality from their parents and surroundings. However, as true as this may be, I believe that we are not only products of our environment, but that we also become products of our thinking. **Proverbs 23:7** says, *"For as he* *thinks in his heart so is he."*

> Carter G. Woodson, historian, author, journalist, and founder of Juneteenth, once said, *"If you can control a man's thinking, you do not have to worry about his action. When you determine what a man shall think, you do not have to concern yourself about what he will do. If you make a man feel that he is inferior, you do not have to compel him to accept an inferior status for he will seek it himself. If you make a man think that he is justly an outcast, you do not have to order him to the back door. He will go without being told; and if there is no back door, his very nature will demand one."*

What a powerful statement! This tells me how powerful the mind is and helps us to understand why so many continue to live beneath their means. By changing our thinking, we ultimately change our lives. The mind can be either our greatest ally or our greatest enemy; our greatest help or our greatest hindrance; our greatest asset or our greatest liability. The mind can work for us or against us. *It all depends on what you feed it.*

Nothing Beats a Failure But a Try

We are tripartite beings: body, soul, and spirit. Our soul is made up of intellect, volition, and emotions. Each component of our being has a designated purpose that is ruled by our spirit. If our spirit man is strong, it will then guide and direct the thought process of the mind. The spirit man will keep the mind in check, because it will always refer the mind back to the Word.

Administrators will recognize mindsets and will spend time encouraging people to "change their thinking." Remember, we operate with grace, and we see how the thought processes of some people have caused them to live a defeated life. We know order and understand that if the *thinking* does not change, the *life* of the person won't either. What is in the mind of someone who makes things happen versus those who don't? Faith and determination! It's a "can do" mindset.

> "I can do all things through Christ who strengthens me."
> **Philippians 4:13**

When we operate out of a "can do" mindset, we know no limitations, boundaries, or intimidations. We realize nothing is too hard for us, and nothing is out of our reach. My mother had a favorite saying, *"Nothing beats a failure but a try."* Then she would say, *"Just try!"* As a young woman, there was never anything I did not think I could do. I would apply for jobs in the workforce that I did not qualify for and would get them. I found myself in management positions, many times being the only one without a degree. A "can do" mindset will try no matter how difficult things look or the appearance of challenges ahead. I am reminded of the words of Edgar Albert Guest, who once wrote a beautiful poem on trying. A portion of it is as follows:

> "Somebody said that it couldn't be done
> But he with a chuckle replied
> That 'maybe it couldn't,' but he would be one
> Who wouldn't say so till he'd tried."

Questions for Reflection

- As an Administrator, we will recognize those around us who are a "product of their own negative thoughts." What are some practical steps that we can take to help someone change their thinking and move from a negative mindset to a positive one?

- Can you point to a time in your life when you overcame an obstacle that seemed insurmountable at the time? As you reflect, think about your mindset at the time—what helped you to rise above your circumstances and emerge victorious?

Action Step

Take some time this week to "feed your mind" with positive words of affirmation. These can be Bible verses, poetry, the words of an author that you admire, or the words of a friend that were spoken at just the right time. Find a journal that will fit in your purse or backpack and carry it with you, so that you are always prepared to write down the words that you will need to hear later.

10

Everyone Matters

When we have the Gift of Administration, we must also acknowledge that the Body of Christ is in need of everyone…and everyone matters! Consider the components of fire: fuel, heat, and oxygen. Now we know that if any of these components are removed, the fire will go out. But there is also a fourth component of fire-—the chemical chain reaction. A chemical chain reaction is required if there is to be a continuous burn.

The Complexity Theory

A *chemical chain reaction* is a series of chemical reactions where everything contributes to the other. The products of the reaction contribute to the reactants of another reaction. In administration and management, there is a term known as the **complexity theory**. Within the complexity theory, there is a "complex adaptive system" where the interactive agents, or all people in the system and Body of Christ, are bound by common goals and needs. In this theory, there is interaction at all levels. In essence, "What you do affects me, and what I do affects you."

For example, if there is a single tree, and that tree catches on fire, it will burn and be consumed, and then the fire will go out, because there is nothing else around it to burn. In contrast, if a tree in the forest catches on fire, it will burn and before long, a chain reaction will occur. A spark, an ember, or flames will soon ignite another tree, and that tree will ignite another; and pretty soon, every tree in the forest, if not controlled, will be on fire. The trees in the forest, although of different heights, types, and purposes, will ignite and burn. Before long, you will have a forest fire.

Paul used the human body to explain and demonstrate the need for unity, harmony, and agreement in diversity that existed in the church. He shared the importance of the complexity theory in the Body of Christ, where the contribution of each member in the body is essential, and interaction with one another is required if the church is going to achieve its common goal. Our common goal is Jesus and advancing the Kingdom of God that He might be glorified. We do not have independent goals—we have one common goal as it pertains to the kingdom. We are all *different*... but we all *matter*.

Paul points out two different personalities or spirits of people in the Body of Christ. Let's look at the language of the first group. **1 Corinthians 12: 15-16**: *"If the foot should say because I am not the hand, I am not of the body, is it therefore not of the body? If the ear should say because I am not an eye, I am not of the body? Is it therefore not of the body? Out of the abundance of the heart the mouth speaks."* So, what is going on in the heart?

The first group Paul deals with are those who have spirits of low self-esteem, feelings of not being good enough, and those with a drawback spirit. There are those who say, "Since I can't do it like him or do it like her, I won't do it at all." When people feel insecure and judged, they prefer to stay out of the public eye in order to avoid being shamed. Those who think, "What am I here for?" or "I have no purpose!" will operate in a state of limbo, forever remaining a "pew or chair member." These people feel insignificant, as though they don't matter. Many are withdrawn and operate as an island. The statement "Because I am not like them, then I am not of the body." verbalizes thoughts that lead to a character of non-participation. This language gives credence to why they feel like they should not actively participate or engage in areas in ministry.

I once heard someone say that the greatest challenges with the body is that it suffers from "comparativeitis."

> *"For we dare not make ourselves of the number or compare ourselves with some that commend themselves: but they are measuring themselves by themselves, and comparing themselves among themselves, are not wise."*
> **2 Corinthians 10:12-13**

There is no need to compare our giftings…who prays the best, who preaches the best, who is the best teacher, who is the best at administration… who's the best…*who's the best*…**who's the best**. Remember…you can only be the best *you* that anyone could ever be. Now just walk it out. If we are not comparing ourselves, we take it to the extreme and compare other's giftings and anointings. We feel that there are only certain people that we are willing to learn from and only certain people that we feel can teach us anything. Yet, it is "out of the mouths of babes and sucklings" that God has ordained strength, so *please do not reject the babes*. We must be careful not to negate our blessing based upon who we feel is "not good enough" for us to listen to.

We ALL Matter

Let us be reminded that *we are all important and matter in the kingdom, for the Lord has need of us all.* It is never about who is the best, but rather always about if and what you are willing to contribute to do your part.

> *"But let each one examine his own work, and then he will have rejoicing in himself alone, and not in another. For each shall bear his own load."*
> **Galatians 6:4-6**

We may be of different genders…but we all matter. We may have attained different educational status…but we all matter. We may be of different income levels…but we all matter. We may be at different spiritual levels…*but we all matter!* We may have different levels of maturity, different spiritual giftings and abilities, and are of different ages. It doesn't matter how different we are…WE. ALL. MATTER!

We all matter because the Lord has placed each of us in the Body of Christ for different purposes and to perform different functions to be used for His glory. The Lord designed the human body and its members, the foot, leg, arm, eyes, ears, nose, etc. Although they are all different, each has a unique purpose and contributes on a different level, and all are equally important. The body is at its best when functioning at maximum capacity. If the eyes are not functioning at 20/20 vision, a correction may be made through a prescription for glasses so that they may function as they have been created to. If the hearing is off and the ears are not functioning at full capacity, we may be given a hearing aid. When a leg is broken, a crutch may provide assistance.

Areas of deficiency are excellent opportunities for the Gift of Administration to cover. The Body of Christ needs everyone operating at full capacity. Therefore, the body needs one with this gift who recognizes that although there are deficiencies, there is still value in a particular area of the body and assistance may need to be prescribed. Never be ashamed to ask for assistance. At one time or another, we all need it. Never before in life did I need reading glasses, but the closer I get to sixty, the more assistance I need to read small print and to even sometimes bring clarity to the larger print. I understood my areas of deficiency and asked for help.

Uniquely Ourselves

When I say, "you matter," what I am really saying is... You are *important*. You are *significant*. You are *relevant*. You *carry weight* and *make a difference* in the Body of Christ. The Apostle Paul says it like this: *"God has set us in the body as He pleased,"* and He does not desire nor expect us to be like someone else. Each one of us has been created to be uniquely who we are. We must get to the place where we recognize the importance of everyone and not just a select few.

In **1 Corinthians 12**, Apostle Paul speaks of those who count themselves unworthy, insignificant, and not needed. Then, in verses **20-22**, he points out another spirit...the *wrong* spirit. He goes from one extreme...those who feel *least* important—to the other extreme—those who feel *most* important. Those with an "all about me" attitude who have no need of anyone else. Let us look at the Word: *"But now indeed there are members, yet one body and the eye cannot say to the hand 'I have no need of you,' nor the head to the feet 'I have no need of you.'"*

Just Like You...Just Like Me

Whether we want to acknowledge it or not, we always have those in the Body of Christ who carry a spirit of pride. If the whole body is like me, and if everyone does it just like me...I really don't *need* anyone. When I was a child, I was a member of the youth usher board of our church. At the close of our weekly meetings, the president would say the following, and each member would repeat it back to him: "If everyone on this usher board were just like me, what kind of an usher board would this usher board be?" We must accept the fact that not everyone is like us and neither do they think like we think.

> *Those of us with the Gift of Administration must always be **mindful** of the differences in others and most importantly, **accept** them.*

I am a fast thinker, fast mover, and (some say) a fast talker. Perhaps I am! However, the truth is that I am still learning to be patient with those who take more time to process things, who move slower than I do and who take two hours to explain something that should take fifteen minutes.

To me, if one is trying to go from Nevada to California, there is a straight route that gets me from point "A" to point "B." I truly do not understand why someone would choose to leave Nevada and head to California by way of New York. (Okay, I told you, I am a work in progress.) I have learned that if I am going to accept *others*, I must first understand and accept *myself*. I must be real with how I think and how I operate. This helps me understand that when someone irritates me, it is not all their fault. The major contributor just may be me. We must practice patience and understanding.

The Spirit of Pride

People with a spirit of pride think that others are not as important as they are and will often surround themselves with those of like minds or those who will serve them and feed their ego. As we observe the human body, we understand that most would think the second toe is not a big deal because there are nine other toes. However, physical therapy evidence shows that if the second toe (or any toe) is amputated, that small missing part will absolutely throw off our balance and compromise our ability to walk and stand.

Oftentimes, prideful people will not recognize that they have a spirit of pride. As one with the Gift of Administration, we must be *aware* of the spirit of pride—and nip it in the bud. Paul understood the importance of recognizing this spirit…and if we do not check it ourselves, you had better believe that the Lord will! In **2 Corinthians 12:7-9,** Paul shares, *"And lest I should be conceited, exalted above measure, prideful, there was given to me a thorn in the flesh…"* Perhaps that thing which is difficult for you to shake has been given to you to keep you humble. Perhaps the stammer in your speech, the limp in your walk, or any part of your struggle, has been allowed so you would not become conceited. I'm just saying…

Scripture lets us know that God *"resists the proud but gives grace to the humble."* Furthermore, *"the Lord detests the proud, and pride comes before a fall."*

> *The Lord desires for us to humble ourselves before Him and in due season, He will exalt us. There is no need for us exalt ourselves.*

Questions for Reflection

- Do you tend to "walk in pride" or "walk in humility?" What do you think others would say about you if you asked them? How do we strike a balance between getting the job done and not coming across as bossy?

- Have you ever taken a personality test such as the Enneagram or the Myers-Briggs? If so, how did the results help you to better understand your administrative giftings?

Action Step

If you have not taken a personality test, spend some time this week doing so. The two most well-known are the Enneagram and the Myers-Briggs. Both are invaluable in helping you to learn how you function and also how to work with those around you who have different personality types.

11

Administrators Never Retreat—We Fight Back!

As Administrators, we must be very careful not to operate with a "Grasshopper Mentality." In **Numbers 13:33**, Moses, with direction from the Lord, sent men out to spy out the land of Canaan, the land flowing with milk and honey, which the Lord said was theirs. Specific commands and instructions were given, and Moses was to choose men from each tribe. Joshua and Caleb were chosen and were instructed to be of good courage and to take the direction of the South. Moses further instructed them to check out the people of the land—were they strong or weak, were there many or few, was the land good or bad, were the cities like camps or strongholds, was the land rich or poor, and were there forests in the land. If there was fruit, they were instructed to bring some back.

A Good Leader Can Strategize

As a good Administrator, Moses gave these directions so that he would know what was ahead of them and could properly strategize to take the land based on their report. A good leader needs to know what they are up against so they can *properly strategize*. While anticipating the good, we must also anticipate hiccups. The spies went out and brought back a report. Yes, the land flowed with milk and honey as the Lord had said. However, the cities were large and fortified, and the people were strong and looked like descendants of Anak; tall, giant, warlike people. There was no way that they could overtake these people—they were bigger and stronger, and they devoured the inhabitants of the land.

Giants represent spirits of intimidation. Intimidation can work on two levels. Not only can we be intimidated *by* people…we can also be the *intimidator*. The best way to deal with a spirit of intimidation is to stand your ground and, if needed, fight back. Don't run…don't retreat…fight back! In **1 Samuel 17**, we find the story of David and Goliath. Goliath, a Philistine, hurled intimidating insults at Saul and his army. He threatened the army of Israel to the point where Saul and his army became afraid at the very appearance of Goliath.

Intimidation at Work

This is a prime example of intimidation at work. I believe there are three forms of witchcraft used to control people. They are manipulation, domination, and intimidation. Manipulation is to *trick* someone into doing what you want them to do; domination is to *force* someone to do what you want them to do; and intimidation is to *frighten* someone into doing what you want them to do. The goal of Goliath's intimidation was to force Israel to serve the Philistines. Israel forgot who they were…and that they were servants of *God* and not of *man*. The Lord said, if we are obedient, we would be the head and not the tail, above only and not beneath. The Israelites were the chosen of God; and yet, they allowed the threats of intimidation to cause them to back down and retreat. Did they not remember who they were? Did they not remember who their God was?

There was a young warrior by the name of David who worked in the field caring for his father's sheep. David had a "backyard anointing" before being anointed king over Israel. He served his father Jesse well and put his life on the line for the sheep. One day, David was asked by his father to take lunch to his brothers who were in the army with Saul. In doing so, David heard the threats of Goliath and observed the men of Israel as they tucked their tails between their legs and ran away. The men of Israel were intimidated by Goliath's threats and feared for their lives.

Now there was sibling rivalry between David and his brothers. Perhaps there was jealousy and envy towards David but needless to say, the first level of warfare and intimidation for David was not with Goliath, but with his brothers. As David arrived on the scene, his oldest brother Eliab, threw verbal punches at David. David's response…"What have I done now?" tells us that this was not the first time words of this magnitude were hurled. The Scripture says David then "turned from him." If we are going to fight words of intimidation, we must turn as David did. By turning, David let his brother know three things:

- He would not allow Eliab's negative words to get into his mind and spirit.
- He would no longer entertain his negative words.
- He would not allow Eliab's negativity to dictate who he was.

I believe we can learn a lesson from David and begin to turn from our accusers. Remember as Paul said, *"By the grace of God I am who I am"* and, (may I add) I am not what you call me or what you think of me!

In the case of Israel's army, they were intimidated by what they heard: the jeering, mocking, and insulting words from Goliath. As with the spies Moses sent out, ten of them allowed what they saw rather than what they heard to intimidate them. They allowed negativity to overrule the positivity. How so? The land was good, flowing with milk and honey and was all God said it was. However, they saw descendants of Anak, tall threatening men, and became intimidated to the point where it caused them to forfeit their promise.

The Grasshopper Mentality

They believed the lie of intimidation, which caused them to see themselves as grasshoppers rather than victorious possessors of the promise. It was disturbing enough that they saw themselves as grasshoppers in their own sight; but now, they were allowing it to determine what they looked like through someone else's eyes. This speaks to the low self-esteem they suffered from. This spirit of intimidation reached the entire congregation also and caused them all to become afraid, thus missing out on the promise.

> We do not know what we look like in someone else's eyes. Therefore, *we need to stop speculating and grab hold of what God says about us.* The grasshopper mentality will make you think less of yourself than you should. The grasshopper mentality will make you forget what God says about you and cause you to take on what others say.

A Different Spirit

What made Caleb and Joshua's testimony different? **Numbers 14:24** tells us that Caleb had a "different spirit." Caleb chose to believe God in the face of adversity and in spite of what his eyes beheld, he walked by faith and not by sight. Caleb and Joshua saw the same things in the land of Canaan as all the other spies did. They saw the good land and its inhabitants. They saw the giants of the land but yet declared, "We can do this!" Caleb immediately calmed and quieted the people and declared, "Let us go up and take possession of the land, for we are well able to overcome it." People like Caleb walk by faith and not by sight. They will *declare it*, and they will *do it*.

Because Caleb refused to retreat, he possessed the promise and his portion of the land at the age of eighty. At forty years old, he believed God was well able to fulfill His promises; and at the age of eighty, he realized the promise. Caleb wanted everything God had spoken over his life. Don't give up, people of God. The deal is still on. The promise is yet at hand. God is not a man that He should lie, nor the son of man that He should repent. If God said it, He shall watch over His Word to perform it.

Caleb, Joshua, and David were warriors and took possession of that which was rightfully theirs. Sometimes, in an effort to protect that which belongs to us, we have to go to war. Sometimes, in order to possess that which is rightfully ours, we have to go to war. Sometimes in an effort to stand against the spirit of intimidation, we have to go to war—and fight back!

Don't Quit!

In **Exodus 17:8-16**, we find the story of the Amalekites, who have picked a fight with Israel. The Amalekites were wicked people who had descended from Esau. They occupied land that belonged to Israel. They were devourers, invasive raiders, and bullies. They harassed and opposed the purpose of the Israelites, therefore, opposing the purpose and will of God. Their attack on Israel was unwarranted and unprovoked. Many reading this message understand what it feels like when it appears the enemy brings an unprovoked attack against you.

The fight was launched to prevent you from obtaining your promise and getting to your destiny. Many times, in the Old Testament, wars between nations and tribes were over possessing territory. Some of our attacks are because we have been promised territory and, in an effort to possess it, the enemy won't just lie down and release it to us. So, we may have to fight in order to possess that which is rightfully ours. Many of you are close to your promise and destiny. *Do not quit now!* Your fight has nothing to do with anything you have done but has come because of who you are and the promise which belongs to you. We understand there are times, as the Scripture says in **Ecclesiastes 10:8**, *"Whoso breaks a hedge, a serpent shall bite him,"* meaning that a breach in one's hedge—be it sin, doubt, or unbelief—can be an open door for the enemy and the cause for attack.

This was not the case with the Amalekites and Israel. The Amalekites picked an unprovoked fight with Israel. Many of us have been taught by our parents not to start fights and not to get involved in the fights of others, but if someone hits you, hit them back.

When we were kids, there was always that one person in our neighborhood who really loved to start fights. Not only did they start fights with others, but they enjoyed bringing division between friends and cause them to fight against each other. They'd start off with jeers like "Ooh, did you hear what so and so said to you?" or "Are you going to take that?" The fights would often start with words and then the instigator would hold out their hand and say,

"Put the meat on the plate and let the hotdog wait." That meant whoever was the boldest and toughest would put their hand on the top of the instigator's hand, promoting a challenge. The other person would then put their hand on top indicating the first hit.

From there, it was on! Those who were friends would now be at war with one another. Interestingly enough, this is what happens in the spirit realm in the church. The enemy causes friendly fire between allies. Nevertheless, no one would sit by and allow a bully or anyone else to just beat up on them. We would always fight back. May I encourage you today to fight back? There has been an unprovoked attack on your life, and you cannot give *up*, give *out*, or give *in*. Too many people are sitting by and being bullied by the enemy. Fight back! Stop letting him pick on you…you *must* fight back!

If we are going to fight back, we must understand some key concepts of the fight:

- **Don't go into battle alone.** Moses orders Israel to fight back, and the first command he gives to Joshua is to choose some men to fight with him. Understanding our battle is a spiritual battle. We must fight in the spirit.
  2 Corinthians 10:4 reminds us "*For the weapons of our warfare are not carnal, but mighty through God to the pulling down of strong holds.*" As we war in this spiritual battle, we must carefully choose those who are well able and qualified to help us to war in the spirit. We need people of prayer and the Word to help us fight. We do not need those who talk a good game and cannot stand under the heat of battle. We do not need those with a gossiping spirit who only want to know your problems so they can share them with everyone else or to use your struggles against you. We need real warriors who will turn down their plates

and help us war in the spirit.

In recent weeks, I was contacted by a Prophet from across the country, and he shared that God was going to expose the Sanballat spirit and secret assassins. Shortly thereafter, I had a pastor and an apostle, both friends and colleagues of mine, contact me regarding dreams they had. In their dreams, the Lord showed them different spirits in operation around me. For one, God showed a Python and a Leviathan spirit; and the other, He showed a spirit of deception. In addition, one of my members had a dream regarding the spirit of intimidation. We could sense the warfare, but we never really knew what we were battling. It appeared everything around us was hit: finances, relationships, and physical bodies. As the Prophet declared, the spirits were and continued to be exposed. It was time to fight back. We organized, chose people to go to war with us, declared a fast for the church, and asked some outside ministry associates to join with us. We began to decree and declare the Word of God over our lives individually as well as corporately. As a result, God began to uncover the hearts of people individually.

Some in leadership came to me and repented for their actions, which included not tithing. As a side note, not tithing is major! If you are in leadership and you are not tithing, you are causing a breech in the hedge. **Ecclesiastes 10:8** says when there is a breech in the hedge, the serpent can come in and bite. If you choose not to tithe, then sit down from leadership because you are cursed with a curse, and you cause the blessings for the ministry to be blocked due to your disobedience. If you are a pastor reading this and you are aware of leaders who are not tithing, sit them down. If they won't obey God, they won't obey you, and they are causing a breech in the ministry.

As a further result of our fasting and declaring the Word of God, bodies were healed, test results came back negative, and revival hit the house. There were even those who left the ministry—which most times, is not a good thing—but we embraced that hidden agendas had been revealed and the perpetrators had to go. As difficult as it was and still is, I had to embrace the "gift of goodbye." We could sense the atmosphere of the ministry had shifted and another level of God's glory was our portion.

- **Don't go into battle empty handed.** Moses told Joshua that he would go, stand on the top of the hill, and take the rod of God with him. Moses did not go empty handed—he went "packing!" He was packing the rod of God. **Ezekiel 20:37** speaks of the rod that shepherds used for their sheep. When the sheep passed under the rod, they were accounted for, examined, and scrutinized. The rod was similar to today's airport scanners which uses electromagnetic waves to determine if there are any suspicious items hidden on a person. As with the scanner, when the sheep passed under the rod, it closely inspected the sheep's wool for anything foreign that should not be there. The rod also represented the Word of God, which has power and authority.

Take Your Position

It was with the rod of God that Moses performed many miracles in Egypt, including the parting of the Red Sea. Moses took it with him to the hill power and authority, miracles, and the wisdom to examine and scrutinize the war that was at hand. Through experience in this battle, Moses recognized that when he held his hands up in victory, his army prevailed in the battle. However, when Moses lowered his hands, the Amalekites triumphed. Could it be that when he raised the rod in his hands, the people who fought below in the battle could behold the rod and remember the prior victories won by the God of the rod? Or, could it be that beholding the rod gave the Israelites a sense of security and hope, knowing that God was with them? Further, could it be that when the rod was lowered and out of sight, the Israelites lost hope? Whatever the case, Moses recognized there was a direct correlation between the holding up of the rod and the Israelites winning the battle.

- **Take your position.** Moses positioned himself on the top of the hill. When Moses was on the backside of the mountain, he had a "backside of the mountain anointing." When Moses was in Egypt, he had an anointing for the Egyptians. When Moses went through his valley experiences, he had the anointing to get him through the valley, but when Moses went to the top of the hill…he had a *hilltop anointing*. This hilltop position allowed him to see every detail of the battle. He positioned himself in the battle in order to have a view so he would not miss anything, and so that he could always be seen.

Those with administrative giftings will always position themselves to see the whole picture.

Administrators know the ins and outs of any assignment. **They look at the whole picture** and know how to strategize in order to get things done. Administrators also understand they cannot always be in the mix, but must sometimes step aside, to change their vantage point.

- **Go into battle prepared.** *Prepared people know their position.* Aaron and Hur went with Moses up to the hilltop. It is not clear if Moses requested Aaron and Hur to go up the hill with him or if they took it upon themselves not to allow their leader to go up the hilltop alone and uncovered. However, what we notice here is that they went with Moses, and they went prepared. We never see where Aaron and Hur murmured or complained because they couldn't fight with Joshua, nor do we hear of the others murmuring and complaining because they couldn't go with Moses. All assumed responsibility for their positions and were prepared for the battle in their own way. We must also note that Moses did not have to pump and prime Aaron and Hur nor did he have to pull them along with him. They went voluntarily. In going with Moses, they were able to anticipate his needs. They were prepared for their mission to ensure their leader was successful in his mission.

Aaron and Hur saw what Moses saw. They recognized there was something supernatural at work and noticed when Moses lifted his hands, the Israelites prevailed; and when he lowered them, the Amalekites prevailed. With one on the right hand of Moses and the other on the left, they held up his arms so that his hands were steady until the end of the battle where Joshua defeated Amalek. In addition, they recognized the weariness of their leader and positioned a rock under him that he might rest himself during the battle.

The Rock That is Higher...

In **Psalm 61:2**, David declares, *"When my heart is overwhelmed, lead me to the rock that is higher than I."* Aaron and Hur helped Moses get to the rock where he would be supported and strengthened. The Rock is Christ Jesus. May I speak to every leader, every intercessor, and every Administrator? You are not just members...you are *kingdom warriors.* Your leader needs you. Stop bickering and jockeying for position. *Stand by your leader's side, lift up their arms, and when needed, help them get to the Rock.* The Israelites prevailed in the battle because they fought back!

Questions for Reflection

- Is there something in your life that you have been praying for, but feel like your prayers are "bouncing off the ceiling?" Just like Moses, we need people to "lift our arms" so that we do not become discouraged and give up. Can you think of two or three people that can be your spiritual "arm lifters?"

- Moses was weary—his leadership roles had worn him out, and he wasn't sure that he had the strength to carry on. Have you ever been at a point in your life where you were just weary? Who were you able to call on to help lift that burden? How long did it take for you to begin to regain your "spiritual strength?"

Action Step

Self-care is so important, and yet most of us are neglecting it. We tell ourselves that things will "fall apart" if we are not right there. Take some time this week to care for yourself. Some ideas include:

- Get a manicure or pedicure.
- Take a long walk by yourself.
- Read a book that has been on your "To Be Read" list.
- Treat yourself to a cup of coffee or tea and a scone.
- Silence your world for an hour. Turn off the phone and the TV, and ask someone to watch the children. Spend an hour in silence, listening for the Lord to speak. Don't give Him an agenda—just listen.

ADMINISTRATION AND GRACE

12

Graceful Administration

It is important for those who operate with the Gift of Administration to do so with grace. People are being damaged by the words and tones of insensitive, prideful people.

Grace to the Humble

If we do not operate in grace, we may become filled with pride, and pride itself becomes a pitfall. According to Strong's Concordance, there are at least five different meanings for the word *grace*. One of the primary uses of grace in the Old Testament is "favor." Noah, Abraham, Lot, Moses, Gideon, and David were just a few who were recipients of the grace and favor of God. **Proverbs 3:4** says we can gain favor with God and favor with man. In the New Testament, this same word *grace* is translated as "unmerited favor." James says this grace is awarded to the humble. Jude tells us grace should not be taken for granted and used as a license to do as one pleases. God's unmerited favor is most amazingly good and by it, we are saved. I am grateful to God that He favors me.

There is, however, another level of grace we must explore. **Hebrews 13:9**: *"For it is good that the heart be established by grace."* The grace referred to here is more than just favor. The meaning here is: "the **merciful kindness** by which God, exerting His holy influence upon souls, **turns** them to Christ, **keeps, strengthens, increases** them in Christian faith, knowledge, affection, and **kindles** them to the exercise of Christian virtues." This grace is not quick to judge and gives way to always being right.

Why Do You Look for What Is Wrong?

When those with the Gift of Administration operate without grace, they will become fault-finders, believing things should be done a certain way—their way—because they know the "right way." As Administrators, we must be extremely careful of this, especially since we do not always know the right or even the best way. Be very careful not to look for faults in people or situations. An example of this: One day, I left home for an appointment and was gone for the majority of the day. I left my husband at home with our two grandchildren, who were seven and ten at the time. I knew how I had left the kitchen and the family room. When I returned, I expected to see everything in order—the same way I left it. I don't leave dishes in the sink or on the counter. We wash dishes as we go along and put them away. The pillows on the family room sofa are in place and everything is orderly.

When I hit the door, I could see that everything was out of order and I began to ask, "Who had this?" or "Who left that out?" My wonderful, gentle, and understanding husband calmly said to me, "Honey, why do you come in and look for things that are wrong?" Who? Me? I wasn't *looking* for anything! It's just that I know how things should be, and for me, it sticks out like a sore thumb when things are out of order. That's the Gift of Administration in me. I have had to learn to choose my battles and decide what is most important. My relationship with my family or my home neatly put together. What would you decide?

When we house the Gift of Administration without grace, we can become insensitive, and neglect the feelings of others; particularly those who feel like they don't measure up to **our** expectations. The last time I checked though, it is *God* who has set the plumb line. We do not have the right to set expectations and require people to live up to them. Let me clarify this. As parents, we have goals, objectives, and expectations for our children. As pastors, we set these for our leadership and members; and as employers, we set them for our employees. We all live with a level of expectation and must clearly communicate such to those we govern. Those of us with the Gift of Administration must exercise grace and meet others where they are. It is so very important that our expectations are not requiring people to become a "mini me." When we get to the point that we become like the judges on shows such as Dancing with the Stars, and have to correct every little effort of people, then we may have crossed the line from administration to judgmental expectation. If we criticize them for not pointing their toes sharply enough or holding their chin up high enough, even though the outcome was a tremendous success, then we have to re-evaluate our perception of grace. We must learn how to embrace them and make them feel important.

Everyone Jesus encountered, from the little children to the woman at the well, were made to feel special. As the Apostle Paul so eloquently stated in **1 Corinthians 19:22**, *"To the weak, became I as weak, that I might win the weak: I have become all things to all men, that I might by all means save some. Now this I do for the gospel's sake, that I may be partaker of it with you."*

Like the Apostle Paul, we must be understanding of man's circumstances and better equip ourselves to deal with them. Our goal should be as his, to become like them in order to win them. As Administrators, we must use the gift of exhortation to encourage and build others up, while remaining sensitive and being careful not to make them feel shameful and discouraged. In doing so, we will win more and retain more.

Lacking Grace...Lacking Understanding

Without grace, people having the Gift of Administration lack understanding. **Proverbs 4:7** says, *"Wisdom is the principal thing; therefore, get wisdom. And in all your getting, get understanding."* Without understanding we will judge, criticize, and become frustrated with people. I told you earlier that those with the Gift of Administration see the big picture. We see how to orchestrate and make things happen. Occasionally, we find that the wrong people have been placed in position and expect them to perform. In working with various people throughout ministry, I am beginning to understand their personalities and capabilities. Everyone who *wants* to do is not always *able* to do. There are others of course, who are well able, but *refuse* to do. In learning people, we must understand their capacity.

There are three "Thinker" types of people we will work with, both in ministry and in our secular jobs. Let us use something as simple as the assignment to clean one's room. The first thinker type we will look at is those you may simply tell to go clean their room. They are *process thinkers* and will know exactly what to do. They will change their sheets or make their bed. They will clean under the bed, check the closet to ensure it is tidy; shoes are on the racks and clothing is on hangers. Everything will be put in its place. They will dust the furniture and vacuum the floor, making sure everything in the room is orderly. With these people, you know you can give them an assignment, and they will explore every option to ensure it is complete.

The second thinker type is those who will willingly go and clean their room, but they must be given specific instructions or a check-off list to work from. Without the specifics, they will clean the room to the best of their ability. However, it may not meet your expectations and more times than not, they will drop the ball somewhere. The bed will be made…but they may not have checked under the bed. The closet door may be closed…but the shoes are disorderly. They may decide to cut corners and choose to either dust or vacuum…but not do both. If you give this group an assignment without specific instructions, you can rest assured that they will do the job, but it will only be half done, leaving more cleanup work for you.

The third thinker is those to whom you will give an assignment to go clean their room and give them a list of things which they must do, but you will have to go over the list with them while sharing the "why" behind doing it. With this type, you may also have to go with them and show them how to do the job properly. Why is that? It is possible that they do not have the capacity to complete the assignment and will approach it with a "stunned deer in the headlights" approach…and the job may never get done. They may spend more time trying to figure it out than you have allotted for the assignment. For these, if the "how to" is left up to them, it will bring confusion, irritation, and frustration to both of you. Understanding people and giving them "grace space" is of utmost importance.

Many with the Gift of Administration are perfectionists and become disgusted with the way things are done if it does not meet their expectations. Oftentimes, they may choose to do it themselves. They may think that no one can do it like they can, so it is best that they just do it, no matter what it is. I have a beautiful eleven-year-old granddaughter who is an Administrator from her heart. She is gifted with discernment and knows who is capable of doing what. She knows order and has insight into the whole picture and how things should be done. That being said, she is a stickler for perfection.

I have someone who comes to help me to do general cleaning on a regular basis. As part of their assignment, they change the beds. One day, after arriving home from school, my granddaughter yelled, "Mimi!" (that's what my grandchildren call me) "Who changed my bed? It's all wrong. The sheets don't line up right, the teal blanket should be next to the sheets, and the tan blanket under the comforter; and what's worse, the comforter is turned the wrong way!" She was upset to the point of tears. She stopped just short of saying, "I will do it all myself. They no longer need to clean my room." She did remake her bed.

As one with the Gift of Administration, my beautiful granddaughter had to learn to operate out of excellence and not perfectionism. There is a difference between excellence and perfectionism. Daniel had a spirit of excellence and because of this knowledge, understanding, problem-solving, and revelation was his.

> "In as much as an excellent spirit, knowledge, understanding, interpreting dreams, solving riddles, and explaining enigmas were found in this Daniel..."
> **Daniel 5:12 (NKJV)**

Excellence is doing well with all of your might and to the best of your ability, whatever your hands find to do. Excellence is accepting, understanding, and learning from your mistakes. Those with the spirit of excellence can make the best out of any situation. Perfectionism gives more credence to things being done perfectly with little regard to effort and no room for mistakes. Perfectionists can set unrealistic goals (expectations) which they themselves cannot always live up to, thus bringing about feelings of unworthiness and inadequacy.

The beautiful part of this story is that after I was able to calm her down and explain grace and patience, she took a notepad and pen, drew a diagram as to how her bed should be made, and wrote very clear and concise instructions. This beautiful little girl has to have her laundry placed in her drawers and hung in her closet a certain way. When laundry is done, her clothes are folded or placed on hangers, and I lay them on her bed so she can put them away. She is extremely organized to the point that all of her clothes are hanging in the closet by type, then by color.

She is excellent with organization, but short on patience. She is a perfectionist and has a very low tolerance for things being out of order. In one sense, it is a good thing that as an Administrator, she won't settle. However, at times, she lacks grace. But with me as her grandmother, she is learning as I am learning.

In contrast, my grandson has the mind of an engineer, and not an Administrator. He sees order as good. However, he is more concerned with linear thinking versus the overall picture. His focus is "bottom line" and often black and white. If you give him specific instructions, he will follow them step by step. It is difficult for him to change up a process or see how things can be done differently, because he follows a format and at times, can be a bit annoyed when things are not done in sequence. Administrators will often think like this; however, this can be very challenging for their call. His thinking is, "If it is not broken, don't fix it." Sounds familiar? If you ever have to work with people who think like this, you must be patient, prayerful, and willing to take the time to work with them.

The lack of grace in any area for the Administrator can cause frustration. A great illustration of this can be found in our ministry where we pray corporately Monday, Wednesday, and Friday mornings at 6 am. There is an order to the prayer: we open with Scripture, have a time of praise and worship, then flow into intercession, and at times, the prophetic. On certain days, we pray from a prayer list with requests from those who have asked us to pray for specific things. Because of the frequent changes to the list, it must be updated regularly, and the updates distributed to the intercessors. This distribution does not always happen as it should.

On one particular morning, one of the intercessors had received a list which had not been updated. When questioned about it, she shared that she was given the list she prayed from at the last minute, and no one told her of the changes. She did not understand why something so simple could be so complicated and commented this caused her to be very annoyed and frustrated. Sounds familiar? Further, she said that she felt like she was the only one who had not received an updated list. Now we have old feelings of rejection and victimization surfacing. She knows how things should be done, and they were not done properly. She was on a roll! As I sat and spoke with this intercessor at length regarding the Gift of Administration, I explained that as an Administrator, one must not only see mistakes and errors, but must exercise their insight to see where the breakdown is and strategize as to how to fix it.

The truth is that she was right, and because she has the Gift of Administration, she was able to determine that things were not handled correctly. The lack of grace caused her to become "annoyed and frustrated." Do you remember how the Gift of Administration is like a helmsman, pilot, and director? Remember the story of Captain Sully Sullenberger who had to deviate from the flight plan because of engine failure?

Administrators must have "Confidence in Chaos." The only way to do this is to operate in grace...and not throw temper tantrums!

Administrators are like helmsmen at control of the wheel and will know how to redirect every situation to get the desired outcome. The one with the Gift of Administration is a problem-solver who looks for solutions. We do not focus on the problems. We do not piggyback on what others have to say about a problem. And neither do we murmur and complain about problems! We are solution-oriented and will always find a solution to the problem at hand.

I am a wife, mother, director of three non-profit organizations, and a pastor. I am raising two of the most beautiful grandchildren ever. My grandchildren are seven and eleven. I am extremely organized with my time because I have to be. I do my own grocery shopping, clean my own home, and usually do all of the cooking. We have set schedules here. Bath time for the kids is 7:30 pm on weeknights. They are in the bed by 8:00 pm in order to give them time to wind down. Their televisions are off at 8:45 pm, and by 9:00 pm, they are asleep. The reason for this is that they must have at least ten hours of sleep before getting up at 7:00 am each morning to get ready for school.

I have school drop-offs and pickups, homeworks to check, spelling tests to give, back-to-school meetings, awards ceremonies, and extracurricular games and events. In addition, I make time for my husband, enjoy fun and games with the kids, counsel with parishioners, pastors, and five-fold ministers, plan and strategize for our ministry, lead prayer lines, teach two Bible studies, and preach two services each week. Get the picture?

With my life, my administrative gifting is one of the best gifts one could ever ask for. Without it, my life would be a shipwreck. I further understand that without the grace afforded to others, I could live a life of judgment, anger, frustration, and discontent. I could very easily give up because it may be perceived as overwhelming.

The life of an Administrator is first and foremost one of prayer. We must stay connected with our Captain, to ensure we are on track and ready to receive needed information in case we have to change course. One thing I know for certain is that God gives us grace to accomplish everything He has assigned to our hands for each season. When He called me, He knew what the events of my life would be like at this moment and time; and yet, He made no exception to the call. He is confident in the oil that He has placed inside me. I am most grateful to my God for understanding me, that I may understand others…and this is all because of His grace.

Questions for Reflection

- Are you a perfectionist, or do you tend to "go with the flow?" Think about your role as Administrator. How does your personality help or hurt you in this role?

- Sometimes, we act differently at home than we do at church or at work. In your role as Administrator, do you function in that role in all areas of your life, or is it something that you view as a "church" thing, that doesn't affect your home and work life?

Action Step

Is there a problem that you are facing right now, at church, work, home, or school, that needs grace and understanding rather than judgment and frustration? How can you use your Gift of Administration to solve the problem, or make the situation better? (Remember—sometimes, the only thing that we can change about a situation is our attitude…and sometimes, that's all it takes!)

References

New King James Study Bible. Second Edition. Earl D. Radmacher, Th.D., Ronald B. Allen, Th.D. Old Testament Editor, H. Wayne House, Th.D., J.D. New Testament Editor. Nashville Tennessee: Thomas Nelson Publishers, 2007. Print.

Carter G. Woodson Quotes. Goodreads.com
Retrieved from:
https://www.goodreads.com/quotes/30798-if-you-can-control-a-man-s-thinking-you-do-not

Yokes. 2018. Merriam-Webster.com
Retrieved from:
https://www.merriam-webster.com/dictionary/yoke

Myles Monroe Quotes. Goodreads.com
Retrieved from:
https://www.goodreads.com/quotes/688275-when-purpose-is-not-known-abuse-is-inevitable

Grace. 2018. Blueletterbible.org
Retrieved from:
https://www.blueletterbible.org/search/search.cfm?Criteria=grace&t=KJV#s=s_primary_0_1

It Couldn't Be Done Poem. 2018. Poetryfoundation.org
https://www.poetryfoundation.org/poems/44314/it-couldnt-be-done

About the Author

Prayer warrior, apostle, prophet, evangelist, pastor, teacher—Dr. Cynthia L. Chess is a multi-gifted leader uniquely fashioned to serve the Body of Christ for such a time as this.

She is the President and Founder of Mountain's Hope Community Worship Center (MHCWC)—one church in three locations: Tracy, Mountain House, and Patterson, California. She is the President and Founder of Victory Over Individual Challenges, Inc. (The VOIC), a Community Economic Educational Development Corporation designed to propel people into their destinies by providing resources focused on prevention, intervention, redemption, and ascension. She is also the President and Founder of both C. L. Chess Ministries and Glory to Glory International Ministries.

As an equipping apostle, God has commissioned and anointed Apostle Chess to plant, multiply, lead, and oversee an apostolic network of churches, ministries, businesses, and leaders. Through her exuberant and inspiring style of preaching and teaching, Apostle Chess equips the saints for the work of the ministry and propels them into their God-given assignments and destiny. As a prophet of God, she also ministers with authority as **Isaiah 58:1** commands, *"Cry aloud and spare not, lift up thy voice like a trumpet and show my people their transgressions and the house of Jacob their sins."*

Apostle Chess is also a successful entrepreneur who is mandated to develop emerging leaders. As a leading authority on

ABOUT THE AUTHOR

understanding and reaching the next generation, Apostle Chess provides multigenerational leadership training and empowerment seminars for churches, public schools, universities, civic organizations, nonprofits, and corporations throughout the United States. She also uses her entrepreneurial expertise and business acumen to cultivate and coach new business owners as they turn their dreams into reality. She believes that "every person can be a leader, because leadership is about influence," and her impartation of this belief has activated giftings and powerfully transformed lives nationwide.

Apostle Chess is a graduate of Shiloh Bible College, E.C. Reems Bible College, and Holy Names College. She was awarded an Honorary Doctor of Ministry Degree from Bell Grove Theological Seminary, on July 31, 2004 and on January 19, 2019, Apostle Chess received her Doctorate in Theology (ThD), from Practical Christian Institute of Evangelism (PCIE). Her community work, which focuses on improving the lives of families, at-risk youth, and the underserved, has garnered her recognition and accolades from the California State Senate and Assembly, the City of Tracy, and many others. She is a recipient of the 2015 Shining Star Award from Preach the Word Worldwide Network in Tallahassee, Florida, which honors and acknowledges those who set the standard as a living testimony in word, deed, and lifestyle and who labor in the ministry of preaching the gospel and simultaneously participate in outreach and mentorship to individuals, their communities, churches, and states.

Apostle Chess resides in Northern California with the love of her life, her husband, Chief Elder Troy. Together, they are changing their city, state, and nation for the glory of God.

Contact the Author

APOSTLE DR. CYNTHIA L. CHESS

213 W. 11th St.

Tracy, CA 95376

(209) 831-2940

admin@clchess.org

http://www.clchess.org

www.ingramcontent.com/pod-product-compliance
Lightning Source LLC
Chambersburg PA
CBHW051406290426
44108CB00015B/2170